Low Carb
Dump Meals

Easy Healthy
One Pot
Meal Recipes

Sarah Spencer

Disclaimer

CONTENTS

INTRODUCTION

At one point in time, eating low carb meant being restrictive. It was about diligently counting carbohydrates, and almost being fearful of adding beautiful, fresh vegetables to your dishes. Today, it is different. There are several very popular low carb eating lifestyles. Some people eat low carb because they love how it makes them feel; others eat low carb because of health concerns and other dietary restrictions. Whatever your reasons for being here, you have made a choice to embark on a dietary lifestyle that has been proven to increase energy and reduce excess weight.

Low carb dump meals highlight flavor and ease. All of the dishes included in this book contain 20 grams or less of net carbs per serving. You will also find a range of calorie content to suit various dietary needs. Some dishes are light and refreshing, while others are rich and comforting. Each and every one uses fresh, wholesome ingredients, including bright, luscious produce that you may have felt shy about using in the past. The freshest of ingredients bring the richest nutritional value to your table, and it is suggested that you always use the freshest and best ingredients that are within your budget.

Dump meals have become popular in recent years as our busy lifestyles have left little time for the simple pleasures such as cooking a meal from scratch. Here, you will see that the days of wholesome real food are not gone forever, but instead made all the easier to achieve. Each dish in this book can also be prepared ahead of time and placed in a container or food storage bag, so that all you need to do is dump and go when you are ready. There is no longer the need to choose between your health and your schedule. I hope that the low carb dump meals included in this book inspire you to reach towards new flavors and to experiment with fresh, beautiful ingredients.

EASY SLOW COOKER WONDERS

Poblano White Bean Chili

Everyone has their favorite white chili recipe. This one is likely to take top place among yours.

Calories: 374   Fat: 18 g   Protein: 27g   Carbs: 19g

Serves: 6

Ingredients:

3 cups cooked chicken, shredded
2 tablespoons olive oil
1 cup red onion, chopped
5 garlic cloves, crushed and minced
1 poblano pepper, seeded and diced
2 15 ounce cans white kidney or cannellini beans, rinsed and drained
3 cups chicken broth
½ cup salsa verde
1 cup Monterey jack cheese, cubed or shredded
½ cup fresh cilantro, diced
1 teaspoon salt
1 teaspoon pepper
1 teaspoon ground cumin
Sliced green onions for garnish, optional
Fresh lime wedges, optional

Directions:

1. Begin by adding the cubed chicken and olive oil to your crock pot. Toss lightly to coat.
2. Add the red onion, garlic, poblano pepper and the two cans of white beans. With a potato masher, press the beans lightly to break some of them up.
3. Add the chicken broth, salsa verde, Monterey jack cheese, cilantro, salt, pepper and cumin. Stir well to make sure all ingredients are blended together.
4. Cook on low for four hours.
5. Serve warm, garnished with fresh green onions and lime wedges, if desired.

Tangy Sesame Chicken for Lettuce Wraps

A bit of an Asian flair with this chicken blends perfectly with the cool lettuce wraps. A special treat with very few net carbs.

Calories: 153   Fat: 5g   Protein: 20g   Carbs: 7g

Serves: 6

Ingredients:

1 pound boneless, skinless chicken breast, cubed
2 teaspoons cornstarch
1 tablespoon sesame oil
1 tablespoon oyster sauce
½ cup soy sauce
¼ cup sugar free ketchup
½ cup chicken stock
2 cups broccoli florets
½ cup red onion, diced
2 cloves garlic, crushed and minced
2 teaspoons fresh ginger, grated
½ teaspoon crushed red pepper flakes
1 tablespoon sesame seeds
6-10 large lettuce leaves for wrapping

Directions:

1. To your crock pot, add the chicken and sprinkle with the cornstarch. Toss lightly to coat the chicken.
2. Add the broccoli, red onion, garlic, ginger, red pepper flakes, and sesame seeds. Toss to mix.
3. Cook on low for 6 hours, or until juices from the chicken run clear.
4. Serve inside large lettuce leaves as a wrap.

Bacon Cheddar Burger Soup

Want a burger? No problem. This soup is rich and has the exact flavors of the perfect burger.

Calories: 543   Fat: 38g   Protein: 30g   Carbs: 17g

Serves: 6

Ingredients:

1 pound ground beef
2 tablespoons tapioca flour
1 cup red onion, diced
1 cup tomatoes, diced
½ cup celery, chopped
½ cup green bell pepper, diced
1 ½ cup sharp cheddar cheese, cubed
8 ounces cream cheese, cubed
4 cups chicken stock
1 cup whole milk
1 tablespoon yellow mustard
4 cloves garlic, crushed and minced
¼ pound cooked bacon, crumbled
1 teaspoon onion powder
1 teaspoon salt
1 teaspoon pepper
Pickle relish, for garnish (optional)

Directions:

1. To your crock pot, add the ground beef and break apart into large chunks. Sprinkle with the tapioca flour and toss to coat.
2. Add the red onion, celery, green bell pepper, cheddar cheese and cream cheese. Toss lightly to mix.

3. Next, add the wet ingredients: the chicken stock, milk, and yellow mustard.
4. Toss in the garlic, crumbled bacon, onion powder, salt, and pepper. Stir and mix well.
5. Cook on low for 4 hours or until ground beef is thoroughly cooked.
6. Garnish with pickle relish if desired.

Italian Spiced Spinach Flank Steak

Flank steak is an often underrated star of the show, but it shines in this dish where it is touched with rich, Italian flavors.

Calories: 328   Fat: 13g   Protein: 33g   Carbs: 16g

Serves: 4

Ingredients:

1 ½ pound flank steak, cut into quarters
1 tablespoon olive oil
1 teaspoon salt
1 teaspoon pepper
1 cup yellow onion, diced
1 cup tomatoes, diced
3 cups fresh spinach, washed and trimmed
½ cup fresh grated parmesan cheese
1 cup beef stock
2 tablespoons balsamic vinegar
1 15 ounce can white beans
2 teaspoons oregano
½ cup fresh basil
4 cloves garlic, crushed and minced

Directions:

1. To the crock pot, add the flank steak quarters and drizzle with olive oil.
2. Sprinkle the steak liberally with the salt and pepper. Toss to coat.
3. Add the yellow onion, tomatoes, and parmesan cheese. Toss gently to mix.

4. Add the beef stock, balsamic vinegar, white beans (including liquid), oregano, basil, and garlic. Toss gently to mix.
5. Cover and cook on low for 6 hours, or until steak is tender and has reached desired doneness.
6. Add the spinach in the last 30 minutes.

Moroccan Slow Cooked Chicken

This recipe has been a standing favorite of our family for many years. The spice blend is a perfect mix for the chicken, the fresh vegetables and chick peas. Sinfully good and low in carbs!

Calories: 593   Fat: 39g   Protein: 42g   Carbs: 17g

Serves: 6

Ingredients:

1 whole chicken, about 3-4 pounds, cut into pieces
1 tablespoon olive oil
½ medium-sized onion, diced
4 cloves garlic, crushed and minced
1 1 teaspoon cumin seeds
1 teaspoon turmeric, ground
1 teaspoon coriander seeds
1 teaspoon ground ginger
1 dash of cayenne pepper, or more to taste
½ teaspoon salt
½ teaspoon pepper
1 15 oz. can diced tomatoes
1 tablespoon tomato paste
1 cup low-sodium chicken stock
3 cups fresh zucchini, cut into chunks
18 cherry tomatoes
1 cup canned chick peas, rinsed

Directions:

1. In a large heavy skillet, warm olive oil over medium-high heat. Sauté onions and garlic for 1 minute, until fragrant. Add chicken and brown on all sides.
2. To the slow cooker, add chicken and onion mixture, cumin seeds, turmeric, coriander seeds, ginger, cayenne pepper, salt, pepper, diced tomatoes, tomato paste, and chicken stock.
3. Toss to mix well. Cover and cook on low for 5 hours
4. After 4 hours and 15 minutes, add zucchini, cherry tomatoes, and chick peas. Continue cooking on low for 45 minutes.

Note: if you are away for the day, set the slow cooker timer to 4 hours and 15 minutes. Upon your return, add zucchini, cherry tomatoes, and chick peas and continue the cooking for another 45 minutes on low or 15-20 minutes on high, until the zucchinis are cooked though. Add some chicken stock if needed.

Chicken and Sage Creamy Casserole

Sage and a rich creamy sauce help this dish feel like home on your plate.

Calories: 360   Fat: 18g   Protein: 34g   Carbs: 12g

Serves: 4

Ingredients:

4 boneless, skinless chicken breasts
1 tablespoon olive oil
3 cups cauliflower florets
1 cup green beans, trimmed
2 cups portabella mushrooms, sliced
1 cup red onion, diced
1 cup chicken stock
3 garlic cloves, crushed and minced
1 teaspoon ground sage
½ teaspoon oregano
1 teaspoon white pepper
½ teaspoon salt
4 ounces cream cheese
½ cup half and half

Directions:

1. Toss the chicken with olive oil and place in the crock pot.
2. Add the cauliflower, green beans, portabella mushrooms, and red onion.

3. Add chicken stock, garlic, sage, oregano, white pepper, and salt. Cover and cook on low for 6 hours.
4. Approximately 30 minutes before serving, remove lid and add the half and half, along with the cream cheese. Stir to mix, replace cover and cook an additional 30 minutes.

Fisherman Stew

Want the perfect low carb dish for a cool evening. The warming flavors of this stew cannot be beat.

Calories: 407   Fat: 16g   Protein: 34g   Carbs: 17g

Serves: 4

Ingredients:

2 15 ounce cans crushed tomatoes with liquid
1 cup sugar free tomato sauce
¼ cup olive oil
1 cup yellow onion, diced
4 cloves garlic, crushed and minced
1 small jalapeno pepper, finely diced
2 ears fresh corn, cut into quarters
½ cup red bell pepper, diced
¼ cup fresh parsley, chopped
¼ cup fresh basil, chopped
1 small sprig fresh rosemary
1 teaspoon thyme
1 teaspoon oregano
1 teaspoon smoked paprika
1 6 ounce salmon fillet, cubed
½ pound medium shrimp, cleaned and deveined
12 scallops
12 mussels

Directions:

1. Begin by combining the crushed tomatoes, tomato sauce, olive oil, yellow onion, garlic, jalapeno pepper, corn quarters, and red bell pepper in your crock pot. Toss gently to mix.

2. Season with the parsley, basil, rosemary, thyme, and oregano. Stir to mix.
3. Cover the crock pot and set to cook on low for 4 hours, until vegetables are tender and broth is fragrant.
4. Approximately 40 minutes before the end time, remove the lid and add all of the seafood. Toss to mix. If you are not satisfied with the amount of broth at this point, you may add additional water or vegetable stock to your liking.
5. Replace the lid and turn the crock pot up to high heat. Allow to cook for 30-40 more minutes or until seafood is cooked and mussels have steamed open.

Pepper and Lime Fajitas

Fresh lime and lettuce wraps make these fajitas light and refreshing.

Calories: 467   Fat: 27g   Protein: 44g   Carbs: 9g

Serves: 4

Ingredients:

1 pound boneless sirloin, cut into strips
2 tablespoons olive oil
1 cup green bell pepper, sliced
1 cup red bell pepper, sliced
1 cup yellow onion, sliced
1 small jalapeno pepper, finely diced
2 cloves garlic, crushed and minced
1 15 ounce can crushed tomatoes, with liquid
1 tablespoon lime juice
2 teaspoons cumin
1 teaspoon paprika
1 teaspoon chili powder
1 teaspoon salt
1 teaspoon pepper
6-8 large lettuce leaves for wrapping
1 avocado, sliced
½ cup queso cheese
1 lime, quartered

Directions:

1. Add the sirloin strips and olive oil to your crock pot. Toss to coat.
2. Add the green and red bell peppers, onion, jalapeno, garlic, canned tomatoes and lime juice. Mix well.

17

3. Season with cumin, paprika, chili powder, salt, and pepper.
4. Cover the crock pot and cook on low for 6 hours, or until beef is tender and has reached desired doneness.
5. Serve in lettuce leaves to wrap, topped with avocado, queso cheese, and lime as garnish.

South of the Border Chicken Posole

The secret ingredient of canned enchilada sauce makes this dump meal one of the most flavorful and easiest to prepare.

Calories: 236   Fat: 6g   Protein: 21g   Carbs: 16g

Serves: 4-6

Ingredients:

3 cups cooked chicken, shredded
2 15 ounce cans green enchilada sauce
2 cups chicken stock
1 15 ounce can white hominy, drained
1 cup shredded carrots
½ cup yellow onion, diced
1 poblano pepper, minced
3 cloves garlic, crushed and minced
¼ cup fresh cilantro, chopped
1 teaspoon ground cumin
1 teaspoon chili powder
1 teaspoon onion powder
1 teaspoon white pepper
1 cup shredded cabbage, for garnish
1 lime, quartered, for garnish

Directions:

1. In your crock pot, combine the shredded chicken, enchilada sauce, and chicken stock. Stir well.
2. Add the white hominy, carrots, onion, poblano pepper, and garlic. Toss to mix.
3. Season with cilantro, cumin, chili powder, onion powder, and white pepper.

4. Cover the crock pot and cook on low for 4 hours.
5. Serve garnished with shredded cabbage and lime quarters.

Creole Seafood

Deeply reminiscent of southern tastes. Use the freshest seafood possible to get the most out of this dish.

Calories: 487   Fat: 22g   Protein: 57g   Carbs: 9g

Serves: 4

Ingredients:

½ pound cooked andouille sausage, sliced
½ cup yellow onion, diced
½ cup green bell pepper, cubed
2 cups vegetable stock
½ cup dry white wine
1 tablespoon tomato paste
4 cloves garlic, crushed and minced
1 ½ teaspoons thyme
1 tablespoon old bay seasoning
1 teaspoon cayenne powder
1 pound medium shrimp, cleaned and deveined
½ pound cod fillets, cubed
½ cup heavy cream

Directions:

1. In a crock pot, combine the andouille sausage, yellow onion, bell pepper, vegetable stock, white wine and tomato paste. Mix well.
2. Season with garlic, thyme, old bay seasoning and cayenne powder.
3. Set crock pot to the lowest setting to cook for 4 hours.

4. After three hours, remove the lid and add the shrimp, cod, and whipping cream.
5. Replace cover and let cook for one hour, or until seafood is cooked thoroughly.

Spicy Peanut Chicken

Simple ingredients are brought to the table to demonstrate what they are capable of in this satisfying dish.

Calories: 407   Fat: 21g   Protein: 7g   Carbs: 11g

Serves: 4

Ingredients:

1 pound boneless, skinless chicken breast, cubed
1 tablespoon olive oil
1 28 ounce can diced tomatoes with liquid
1 cup chicken stock
½ cup natural peanut butter, either creamy or chunky
½ cup yellow onion, diced
2 cups cauliflower florets
3 cloves garlic, crushed and minced
1 jalapeno pepper, finely diced
1 tablespoon fresh lemongrass
1 teaspoon cumin
½ teaspoon crushed red pepper flakes
¼ teaspoon cinnamon
½ teaspoon salt
½ teaspoon pepper
Chopped peanuts for garnish

Directions:

1. In a crock pot, combine the cubed chicken breast and the olive oil. Toss to coat.
2. Add the diced tomatoes, chicken stock, and peanut butter. Mix well.

3. Add the yellow onion, cauliflower, garlic, and jalapeno pepper. Toss to mix.
4. Season with fresh lemon grass, cumin, crushed red pepper flakes, cinnamon, salt and pepper.
5. Cover and cook on low setting for 6 hours.
6. Garnish with chopped peanuts before serving.

Red Curried Beef

Curry, when used just right, is one of the most beautiful flavors in the world. In this dish beef is elevated with tantalizing flavors.

Calories: 335   Fat: 18g   Protein: 29g   Carbs: 11g

Serves: 6

Ingredients:

1 ½ pound flank steak, cut into strips
1 tablespoon olive oil
1 cup yellow onion, diced
1 15 ounce can diced tomatoes
1 tablespoon tomato paste
1 14 ounce can unsweetened coconut milk
2 cups beef stock
¼ cup soy sauce
1 tablespoon lime juice
3 cloves garlic, crushed and minced
1 tablespoon fresh ginger, grated
1 tablespoon lemongrass, chopped
½ teaspoon cinnamon
1 teaspoon red curry paste
1 teaspoon ground coriander
2 cups broccoli florets
2 cups cauliflower florets
½ cup carrots, diced
2 cups bok choy, coarsely sliced

Directions:

1. To your crock pot, add the sliced steak and olive oil. Toss to coat.
2. Add the yellow onion, canned tomatoes, tomato paste, coconut milk, beef stock, soy sauce, and lime juice. Stir to mix well.
3. Season with the garlic, fresh ginger, lemongrass, cinnamon, red curry paste, and coriander. Stir to incorporate.
4. Add the broccoli, cauliflower, carrots, and bok choy. Toss to mix.
5. Cover the crock pot and cook on low for 6 hours, or until vegetables are tender and meat has reached desired doneness.

Grilled Cheese Tomato Soup

All of the flavor of the favorite combination without any of the bread.

Calories: 300   Fat: 19g   Protein: 15g   Carbs: 13g

Serves: 6

Ingredients:

2 28 ounce cans crushed fire roasted tomatoes
1 tablespoon tomato paste
1 tablespoon honey
4 cups chicken stock
¼ pound cooked bacon, crumbled
1 cup red onion, chopped
½ cup red bell pepper, diced
1 sprig fresh rosemary
1 sprig fresh thyme
1 teaspoon black pepper
1 teaspoon salt
½ cup fresh basil, chopped
4 ounces cream cheese
½ cup Gruyere cheese
½ cup heavy cream

Directions:

1. To your crock pot, add the canned tomatoes, tomato paste, honey, and chicken stock. Stir to combine.
2. Add the bacon, red onion, and red bell pepper. Toss gently.
3. Season with rosemary, thyme, black pepper, salt, and basil.

4. Place lid on crock pot and cook on low for two hours or until broth has cooked down slightly and flavors have blended.
5. Add the cream cheese, Gruyere cheese and heavy cream. Stir, replace cover and cook for an additional 30 minutes.
6. Garnish with additional fresh basil, if desired.

Balsamic Brisket

Balsamic vinegar makes everything better, which is proven in this tender brisket dish.

Calories: 467   Fat: 24g   Protein: 50g   Carbs: 8g

Serves: 6

Ingredients:

1 2 pound beef brisket
2 tablespoons olive oil
1 ½ cup red onion, sliced
3 cups wild mushroom mix, sliced
½ cup celery sliced
1 cup green beans, cleaned and trimmed
1 cup cherry tomatoes, quartered
5 cloves garlic, crushed and minced
½ cups balsamic vinegar
4 cups beef stock
2 bay leaves
2 teaspoons fresh ground black peppercorns
1 teaspoon thyme
1 teaspoon oregano
1 teaspoon salt
Green onions, sliced, for garnish

Directions:

1. Coat the brisket with olive oil and place in a crock pot, cutting the meat into several pieces if necessary for fit.
2. Top the brisket with the red onion, mushrooms, celery, green beans, cherry tomatoes, and garlic.
3. Pour in the balsamic vinegar and beef stock. Stir well.

4. Season with bay leaves, black peppercorns, thyme, oregano, and salt.
5. Cover and cook on low for at least 6 hours, or until meat is tender and has reached the desired doneness. Check periodically for moisture content and add more beef stock if needed.
6. Serve garnished with green onions, if desired.

ONE BOWL SALADS AND CHILLED DISHES

Crunchy Chicken and Broccoli Salad Bowl

This broccoli salad is full of flavor and just the right amount of crunch. Plus it packs a powerful protein punch.

Calories: 715   Fat: 40g   Protein: 37g   Carbs: 14g

Serves: 4 as a light meal

Ingredients:

½ cup plain yogurt
½ cup light mayonnaise
½ cup apple cider vinegar
2 teaspoons honey
1 tablespoon fresh basil, chopped
½ teaspoon paprika
1 teaspoon salt
1 teaspoon pepper
2 cups cooked chicken, cubed
1 cup cooked bacon, crumbled
3 cups broccoli florets
½ cup red onion, finely diced
1 cup cherry tomatoes, quartered
½ cup radishes, sliced
1 cup peanuts, chopped
1 cup aged cheddar cheese, shredded

Directions:

1. In a large salad bowl, combine the yogurt, mayonnaise, apple cider vinegar, honey, basil, paprika, salt, and pepper. Whisk until well blended and slightly emulsified.
2. Add the chicken, bacon, broccoli, red onion, cherry tomatoes, and radishes. Toss to coat with dressing.
3. Add the peanuts and cheddar cheese. Toss just enough to mix.
4. Place in the refrigerator and allow to chill for two hours before serving.

Seven Layer Italian Salad

This salad offers a slightly different take on a traditional salad. Think of this recipe the next time you need to bring a dish to pass.

Calories: 454   Fat: 27g   Protein: 27g   Carbs: 15g

Serves: 6 as a meal

Ingredients:

½ cup mayonnaise
½ cup sour cream
1 tablespoon balsamic vinegar
1 tablespoon fresh basil, finely chopped
1 teaspoon salt
1 teaspoon pepper
4 cups fresh spinach, cleaned, dried and torn into large pieces
4 cups romaine lettuce
½ pound cooked bacon, crumbled
1 cup ham, cubed
1 cup sopressata sausage, cubed
6 hard-boiled eggs, chopped
2 cups lima beans, cooked and drained
2 cups Roma tomatoes, diced
5 green onions, sliced
1 cup provolone cheese, shredded

Directions:

1. In a large salad bowl, combine the mayonnaise, sour cream, vinegar, basil, salt, and pepper. Whisk until well blended and spread evenly along the bottom of the bowl.

2. Create the greens layer by adding the spinach and romaine lettuce in a layer on top of the dressing.
3. For the meat layer, combine the bacon, sopressata, and ham, and layer over the greens.
4. Next add the eggs, lima bean, and Roma tomatoes in layers.
5. Top with sliced green onions and provolone cheese.
6. Chill for two hours before serving.

Strawberry and Herb Dump Salad

A little sweet and a little savory. The perfect way to highlight fresh seasonal strawberries.

Calories: 314   Fat: 26g   Protein: 12g   Carbs: 7g

Serves: 4 as a meal

Ingredients:

¼ cup olive oil
1 tablespoon lime juice
1 teaspoon salt
1 teaspoon pepper
½ teaspoon thyme
4 cups baby spinach, torn
½ cup fresh basil, chopped
½ cup fresh parsley, chopped
¼ cup fresh mint, chopped
1 ½ cups strawberries, sliced
1 cup cooked beets, diced
1 cup walnuts, coarsely chopped
½ cup goat cheese, crumbled

Directions:

1. In a large salad bowl, combine the olive oil, lime juice, salt, pepper, and thyme. Whisk until well blended and slightly emulsified.
2. Add the spinach, basil, parsley, and mint. Toss to coat.
3. Add the strawberries, beets, and walnuts. Toss gently.
4. Top with goat cheese and place in the refrigerator for at least one hour to chill before serving.

Sugar Pea and Kale Salad with Smoky Vinaigrette

Crunchy kale and a light smokiness pair perfectly with the sweet delicacy of sugar peas.

Calories: 477   Fat: 42g   Protein: 15g   Carbs: 9g

Serves: 4 as a meal

Ingredients:

½ cup extra virgin olive oil
3 tablespoons rice vinegar
1 teaspoon smoked paprika
1 tablespoon fresh tarragon
1 teaspoon salt
1 teaspoon pepper
4 cups kale, chopped
¼ cup fresh mint, chopped
2 cups sugar snap peas, trimmed
1 cup crispy pancetta, chopped
½ cup walnuts chopped
½ cup feta cheese, crumbled

Directions:

1. In a large salad bowl, combine the olive oil, rice vinegar, smoked paprika, tarragon, salt, and pepper. Whisk well to blend.
2. Add the kale, mint, sugar snap peas, pancetta, and walnuts. Toss to coat with dressing.
3. Top with feta cheese and allow to chill one hour before serving.

Easy Tossed Cobb Salad

Cobb salads are notorious for being rich and filling, but the layers add time and energy to the preparation. This one dish salad skips on none of the flavor, but will save you valuable time.

Calories: 644   Fat: 48g   Protein: 40g   Carbs: 7g

Serves: 4 as a meal

Ingredients:

¼ cup extra virgin olive oil
2 tablespoons balsamic vinegar
1 tablespoon lemon juice
1 teaspoon stone ground mustard
1 clove garlic, crushed and minced
½ teaspoon salt
1 teaspoon pepper
6 cups romaine lettuce, chopped
1 cup watercress, chopped
3 hard-boiled eggs, chopped
2 cups cooked chicken, cubed
½ cup crispy pancetta, chopped
1 avocado, cubed
1 cup tomato, chopped
½ cup cucumber, chopped
1 cup gorgonzola cheese, crumbled

Directions:

1. In a large salad bowl, combine the olive oil, balsamic vinegar, lemon juice, stone ground mustard, garlic, salt, and pepper. Whisk until well blended and slightly emulsified.

2. Add the romaine lettuce and watercress. Toss to coat with dressing.
3. Add the eggs, chicken, pancetta, avocado, tomato, cucumber, and gorgonzola cheese. Toss to mix.
4. Serve immediately or allow to chill for one hour.

Chilled Garlic Shrimp and Spring Vegetable Bowl

Reminiscent of shrimp scampi, but chilled and perfect for a warm, sunny day.

Calories: 258   Fat: 15g   Protein: 26g   Carbs: 4g

Serves: 4

Ingredients:

1 pound medium cooked shrimp
¼ cup extra virgin olive oil
1 tablespoon lemon juice
1 tablespoon fresh lemongrass
1 teaspoon salt
1 teaspoon pepper
3 garlic cloves, crushed and minced
1 medium bunch asparagus spears, stems removed, sliced thinly lengthwise
1 cup snow peas, trimmed
½ cup radish, sliced thin
½ cup spring onions, sliced

Directions:

1. In a large bowl, combine the olive oil, lemon juice, lemongrass, salt, pepper, and garlic. Whisk until well blended.
2. Add the shrimp, asparagus, snow peas, and radishes. Toss to coat.
3. Top with spring onions and chill at least two hours before serving.

Smoked Salmon and Avocado Bowl

The smokiness of salmon and the creaminess of avocado complement each other perfectly in this easy, flavorful bowl.

Calories: 622   Fat: 47g   Protein: 29g   Carbs: 9g

Serves: 4

Ingredients:

½ cup extra virgin olive oil
3 tablespoons lemon juice
1 teaspoon stone ground mustard
1 tablespoon honey
1 teaspoon salt
1 teaspoon coarse ground black pepper
4 cups spinach, torn
1 cup arugula, torn
1 cup radish, thinly sliced
1 cup edamame, cooked
1 pound smoked salmon, thinly sliced
1 avocado, sliced
½ cup goat cheese, crumbled
1 tablespoon capers
1 tablespoon fresh dill

Directions:

1. In a large bowl, combine the olive oil, lemon juice, mustard, honey, salt, and pepper. Whisk until well blended and slightly emulsified.
2. Add the spinach and toss to coat.
3. Add the radish, edamame, smoked salmon, goat cheese, capers, and dill. Toss to mix.

Caprese Toss Bowl

This traditional low carb Italian salad is brightened with a few extra special ingredients.

Calories: 390   Fat: 29g   Protein: 16g   Carbs: 11g

Serves: 4

Ingredients:

3 cucumbers, chopped
2 cups cherry tomatoes, halved
2 avocados, diced
½ cup fresh basil, coarsely chopped
2 cups small fresh mozzarella balls
½ cup red onion, diced
1 teaspoon salt
1 teaspoon pepper
1 tablespoon extra-virgin olive oil
2 tablespoons balsamic vinegar

Directions:

1. In a large salad bowl, combine the cucumbers, cherry tomatoes, avocados, basil, mozzarella, and red onion. Toss gently to mix.
2. Sprinkle with salt and pepper and then drizzle with the olive oil and vinegar. Toss gently to coat.
3. Serve immediately or chill one hour before serving.

Buffalo Blue Chopped Salad Bowl

If you love buffalo wings and blue cheese, but need to skip the breading and sugar laden dressings, this salad is sure to please.

Calories: 586   Fat: 40g   Protein: 30g   Carbs: 18g

Serves: 4

Ingredients:

1 cup mayonnaise
1 tablespoon powdered ranch dressing seasoning mix
1 tablespoon cayenne pepper sauce
2 tablespoon fresh lemon juice
4 cups romaine lettuce, chopped
2 cups cooked chicken, cubed
½ cup cooked bacon, chopped
½ cup canned black beans, rinsed and drained
1 cup Roma tomato, diced
½ cup cashews, chopped
1 avocado, diced
½ cup blue cheese, crumbled
¼ green onion, sliced

Directions:

1. In a large salad bowl, combine the mayonnaise, ranch seasoning mix, cayenne pepper sauce, and lemon juice. Whisk until blended.
2. Add the romaine lettuce, chicken, and bacon. Toss to coat with the dressing.
3. Add the Roma tomatoes, cashews, avocado, and blue cheese. Toss to mix.
4. Top with green onion and serve immediately or chill for one hour before serving.

DUMP IT IN THE OVEN AND GO

Low Carb Deep Dish Pizza

Pizza does not need to be a thing of the past. This pizza casserole takes 5 minutes to prepare and will remind you that you are not missing anything on your low carb diet.

Calories: 514   Fat: 32g   Protein: 37g   Carbs: 15g

Serves: 8

Ingredients:

1 pound smoked ham, cubed
½ pound pepperoni, sliced
1 cup portabella mushrooms, sliced
1 cup red bell pepper, chopped
1 cup red onion, diced
½ cup fresh pineapple cut into small chunks
4 cloves garlic, crushed and minced
1 10 ounce can pizza sauce
½ cup fresh basil, chopped
1 teaspoon oregano
1 teaspoon rosemary
1 teaspoon salt
1 teaspoon pepper
2 cups mozzarella cheese, shredded
1 cup provolone cheese, shredded
¼ cup parmesan cheese, shredded

Directions:

1. Preheat oven to 425°F.
2. In a 9x13 inch baking dish, add the ham, pepperoni, mushrooms, red bell pepper, red onion, and pineapple. Toss to mix.
3. Add the garlic, pizza sauce, fresh basil, oregano, rosemary, salt, and pepper. Stir to mix well and coat all ingredients.
4. Cover with mozzarella cheese, provolone cheese, and parmesan cheese.
5. Place in the oven and bake for 20-25 minutes until cheese is melted and bubbly.
6. Serve warm.

Chicken Florentine

This version of chicken Florentine is easy to prepare and will satisfy even the most carb restrictive of diets.

Calories: 513   Fat: 33g   Protein: 38g   Carbs: 8g

Serves: 4

Ingredients:

1 tablespoon olive oil
2 10 ounce packages frozen spinach, thawed and drained
½ cup red onion, diced
1 teaspoon crushed red pepper flakes
4 boneless skinless chicken breasts, sliced
5 tablespoons butter, cubed
3 cloves garlic, crushed and minced
1 sprig fresh rosemary, stem removed
½ cup dry white wine
½ cup heavy cream
½ cup freshly grated parmesan cheese
1 tablespoon chopped fresh Italian parsley

Directions:

1. Preheat oven to 375°F.
2. Coat the bottom of a 9x13 inch baking dish with olive oil.
3. Add the spinach, red onion, and crushed red pepper flakes. Toss lightly to mix.
4. Top the spinach with slices of chicken, cubed butter, garlic, rosemary, white wine, heavy cream, and parmesan cheese. Gently stir just enough to make sure some of the liquid has reached the spinach.

5. Place in the oven and bake for 40-45 minutes, or until chicken juices run clear.
6. Garnish with fresh parsley before serving.

Caribbean Pork Bake

A taste of the Caribbean dresses up otherwise typical pork with exotic flavors.

Calories: 455   Fat: 30g   Protein: 28g   Carbs: 14g

Serves: 4

Ingredients:

1 pound boneless pork, cubed
2 cups acorn squash, cubed
2 cup red bell pepper, chopped
1 cup fresh pineapple chunks
2 tablespoons soy sauce
¼ cup Worcestershire sauce
2 tablespoons sugar free orange juice
1 tablespoon olive oil
3 cloves garlic, crushed and minced
1 tablespoon fresh ginger, grated
1 teaspoon allspice
1 teaspoon crushed red pepper flakes
1 teaspoon salt
1 teaspoon pepper

Directions:

1. Preheat oven to 425°F.
2. In a 9x13 inch baking dish, combine the pork, acorn squash, red bell pepper, and pineapple chunks. Toss to mix.
3. Add the soy sauce, Worcestershire sauce, orange juice and olive oil. Stir and toss to coat.

4. Season with the garlic, allspice, crushed red pepper flakes, salt, and pepper. Toss to season throughout.
5. Place in the oven and bake for 40-45 minutes or until pork is cooked through and vegetables are tender.

Herb and Wine Dump Chicken with Vegetables

When you are craving a rich, elegant meal but want none of the fuss, this chicken dish will do the trick.

Calories: 300   Fat: 11g   Protein: 34g   Carbs: 4g

Serves: 4

Ingredients:

2 tablespoons olive oil
1 ½ pounds chicken breasts and thighs
2 cups asparagus tips
1 cup button mushrooms, sliced
1 cup dry red wine
2 cloves garlic, crushed and minced
2 shallots, sliced thin
1 sprig fresh rosemary
¼ cup fresh basil, chopped
1 teaspoon thyme
1 teaspoon salt
1 teaspoon cracked black peppercorn
1 orange, sliced

Directions:

1. Preheat oven to 350°F.
2. In a 9x13 inch baking dish combine the chicken, asparagus and mushrooms. Toss with olive oil to coat.
3. Add the red wine, garlic, rosemary, basil, thyme, salt, and cracked black peppercorn. Toss to coat.

4. Top dish with orange slices.
5. Place in the oven and bake for 45-50 minutes, or until chicken juices run clear.

Spicy Citrus Chicken

A touch of spice takes the tart out of the citrus in this dish, leaving nothing but perfectly blended flavors.

Calories: 257   Fat: 11g   Protein: 38g   Carbs: 4g

Serves: 4

Ingredients:

1 ½ - 2 pounds boneless, skinless chicken breast
2 cups Brussels sprouts, halved
2 tablespoons olive oil
¼ cup orange juice, no sugar added
1 tablespoon fresh lime juice
1 tablespoon orange zest
1 small jalapeno pepper, diced
2 tablespoons smoked paprika
¼ teaspoon cayenne powder
1 teaspoon salt
1 teaspoon white pepper
1 lemon, sliced

Directions:

1. Preheat oven to 350°F.
2. In a 9x13 inch baking dish, combine the chicken and Brussels sprouts. Drizzle with olive oil and toss to coat.
3. Add the orange juice, lime juice, orange zest, and jalapeno pepper. Toss to mix.
4. Season with smoked paprika, cayenne powder, salt, and white pepper. Top with lemon slices.
5. Place in the oven and bake for 45-50 minutes, or until chicken juices run clear.

Low Carb Blueberry Breakfast Crumble

When you are craving something a little sweet, this crumble highlights the sweetness of fresh berries with only 12 g of carbs per serving.

Calories: 198   Fat: 10g   Protein: 14g   Carbs: 12g

Serves: 10

Ingredients:

2 cups fresh blueberries, washed and dried
½ cup oat flour
½ cup vanilla whey powder
1 tablespoon orange juice, no sugar added
2 teaspoons cinnamon
1 teaspoon nutmeg
¼ cup sugar substitute, such as stevia
¼ cup butter, cut into very small cubes
½ cup rolled oats

Directions:

1. Preheat oven to 350°F.
2. Lightly oil a 9x9 inch baking dish.
3. Add blueberries, oat flour, vanilla whey powder, orange juice, cinnamon, nutmeg, and sugar substitute. Toss to mix, until berries are coated.
4. Top with cubed butter and rolled oats.
5. Place in the oven and bake for 30-35 minutes, or until berries are tender.

Easy Breakfast Casserole

Easy mornings are not all about pancakes and waffles. This breakfast is almost as easy as popping a frozen pastry in the toaster.

Calories: 285   Fat: 18g   Protein: 27g   Carbs: 5g

Serves: 4

Ingredients:

8 eggs
1 tablespoon milk or heavy cream
1 tablespoon fresh dill, chopped
2 teaspoons fresh rosemary
1 teaspoon salt
1 teaspoon pepper
½ cup cottage cheese
½ cup fontina cheese, cubed
1 cup smoked ham, cubed
1 cup white mushrooms, sliced
1 cup red bell pepper, sliced

Directions:

1. Preheat oven to 350°F.
2. Lightly oil a 9x13 inch baking dish
3. Crack the eggs into the baking dish and add the milk, dill, rosemary, salt, and pepper. Whisk until blended and eggs are creamy.
4. Place the cottage cheese in small dollops into the baking dish, top with fontina cheese, ham, mushrooms and red bell pepper. Gently shake the dish back and forth to settle some of the ingredients.

5. Place in the oven and bake 35-40 minutes, or until eggs are set in the middle.
6. Let rest for at least 5 minutes before serving.

Savory Mushroom Casserole

A mushroom medley takes on the form of comfort food in this rich, satisfying casserole.

Calories: 503   Fat: 45g   Protein: 17g   Carbs: 10g

Serves: 4

Ingredients:

2 cups portabella mushrooms, sliced
1 cup button mushrooms, sliced
1 cup porcini mushrooms, sliced
1 tablespoon olive oil
1 cup leeks, sliced, white parts only
2 cups fresh spinach, torn
½ cup red onion, diced
1 cup gruyere cheese, shredded
¼ cup fresh grated parmesan
1 cup heavy cream
1 teaspoon nutmeg
1 teaspoon salt
1 teaspoon pepper
½ cup walnuts, chopped

Directions:

1. Preheat oven to 375°F.
2. Lightly oil a 9x9 inch baking dish.
3. To the baking dish, add the three varieties of mushrooms and drizzle with olive oil. Toss to coat.
4. Add the leeks, spinach, red onion, gruyere cheese, and parmesan cheese. Toss to mix.

5. Pour the heavy cream over the mushrooms and season with nutmeg, salt, and pepper. Stir to mix well.
6. Top with chopped walnuts.
7. Place in the oven and bake for 20-25 minutes, or until mushrooms are tender.
8. Let rest at least 5 minutes before serving.

Spaghetti Squash Carbonara

From time to time you may get a craving for a savory, carb loaded meal. This carbonara will completely satisfy that craving with none of the guilt.

Calories: 441   Fat: 17g   Protein: 40g   Carbs: 17g

Serves: 4

Ingredients:

4 cups cooked spaghetti squash
½ pound crispy pancetta, diced
2 cups peas, fresh or frozen
1 cup red onion, diced
2 cloves garlic, crushed and minced
½ cup dry white wine
4 eggs, beaten
½ cup ricotta cheese
1 cup fresh grated parmesan cheese
1 teaspoon salt
1 teaspoon black pepper
½ cup fresh parsley, chopped

Directions:

1. Preheat oven to 350°F.
2. Lightly oil a 9x13 inch baking dish.
3. Add the spaghetti squash, pancetta, peas and onion to the dish. Toss to mix.
4. Pour in white wine and eggs. Top with ricotta cheese, parmesan cheese, salt, pepper, and parsley. Toss to mix.
5. Place in the oven and bake 40 minutes, until casserole is bubbly.
6. Let rest 5-10 minutes before serving.

Wine and Olive Chicken

This is the perfect combination of flavor and texture that brightens up the standby chicken beast.

Calories: 459   Fat: 28g   Protein: 34g   Carbs: 8g

Serves: 4

Ingredients:

1 ½ - 2 pounds boneless, skinless chicken breast
2 tablespoons olive oil
1 cup yellow onion, diced
1 cup cherry tomatoes, quartered
4 cloves garlic, crushed and minced
1 cup olives (any variety), halved
1 cup dry white wine
½ cup heavy cream
1 tablespoon fresh thyme
1 sprig fresh rosemary
1 teaspoon salt
1 teaspoon pepper

Directions:

1. Preheat oven to 350°F.
2. Lightly oil a 9x13 inch baking dish.
3. Add the chicken breast and drizzle with oil. Toss to coat.
4. Add the onion, cherry tomatoes, garlic, and olives. Toss to mix.
5. Pour in the white wine and heavy cream. Season with thyme, rosemary, salt, and pepper.
6. Place in the oven and bake for 45-55 minutes, or until chicken juices run clear.

Chicken Cordon Blue Bake

This deconstructed version of the famous dish highlights all of the flavors with very few carbs.

Calories: 300   Fat: 11g   Protein: 38g   Carbs: 6g

Serves: 6

Ingredients:

2 pounds boneless, skinless chicken breast, cubed
1 cup smoked ham, diced
½ cup red onion, diced
1 cup button mushrooms, sliced
3 cloves garlic, crushed and minced
½ cup dry white wine
1 cup whole milk
1 egg, beaten
1 cup Swiss cheese, cubed
1 teaspoon thyme
1 teaspoon tarragon
1 teaspoon salt
1 teaspoon pepper

Directions:

1. Preheat oven to 350°F.
2. Lightly oil a 9x13 inch baking dish.
3. Add the chicken, ham, red onion, mushrooms, and garlic. Toss to mix.
4. Pour in the white wine, milk, and egg. Toss to mix.

5. Add Swiss cheese, thyme, tarragon, salt, and pepper. Stir to make sure seasoning is spread throughout.
6. Place in the oven and bake for 40-45 minutes, or until chicken juices run clear.

One Dish Brilliant Morning Breakfast

A rich, flavorful one dish breakfast that is an easy crowd pleaser.

Calories: 341   Fat: 26g   Protein: 19g   Carbs: 7g

Serves: 6

Ingredients:

1 pound sage breakfast sausage, cooked and crumbled
2 cups leeks, sliced, white parts only
1 cup tomato, diced
1 cup arugula
1 cup aged cheddar, cubed
1 cup Swiss cheese, cubed
¼ teaspoon cayenne powder
½ teaspoon salt
1 teaspoon pepper
6 eggs, beaten
½ cup heavy cream

Directions:

1. Preheat oven to 375°F.
2. Lightly oil a 9x9 baking dish.
3. Add the sausage, leeks, tomatoes, and arugula. Toss to mix.
4. Add the cheddar cheese, Swiss cheese, cayenne powder, salt, and pepper. Toss to mix.
5. Pour eggs and heavy cream into the dish. Stir slightly.
6. Place in the oven and bake for 35-40 minutes, or until eggs are completely set.

Cauliflower Mac and Cheese

You don't need to give up all of your old carb loaded favorites. Cauliflower replaces pasta in this rich, low carb dish.

Calories: 427   Fat: 32g   Protein: 24g   Carbs: 10g

Serves: 4

Ingredients:

1 large head cauliflower, cut into small florets
½ cup cream cheese
1 cup sharp cheddar
½ cup gruyere cheese
½ cup blue cheese, crumbled
1 cup heavy cream
2 teaspoons Dijon mustard
2 cloves garlic, crushed and minced
1 teaspoon nutmeg
1 teaspoon salt
1 teaspoon pepper
2 Roma tomatoes, sliced

Directions:

1. Preheat oven to 350°F.
2. Lightly grease a 9x9 baking dish.
3. Add the cauliflower, cream cheese, cheddar cheese, gruyere cheese, and blue cheese. Toss to mix.
4. Pour in heavy cream and season with Dijon mustard, nutmeg, salt, and pepper. Toss gently to mix well. Top with slices of Roma tomatoes.
5. Place in the oven for 40-45 minutes, or until cauliflower is tender.

Hawaiian Island Bake

Escape away to the islands with some of these traditional Hawaiian flavors.

Calories: 227   Fat: 5g   Protein: 28g   Carbs: 14g

Serves: 6

Ingredients:

1 pound boneless skinless chicken, cubed
½ pound smoked ham, cubed
1 cup red onion, diced
2 cups acorn squash, cubed
1 cup red bell pepper sliced
1 ½ cups fresh pineapple chunks
3 cloves garlic, crushed and minced
1 tablespoon fresh ginger, grated
1 cup orange juice, no sugar added
¼ cup soy sauce
1 tablespoon honey
1 teaspoon salt
1 teaspoon pepper

Directions:

1. Preheat oven to 350°F.
2. Lightly oil a 9x13 inch baking dish.
3. Add chicken, ham, red onion, acorn squash, red bell pepper, pineapple, garlic, and ginger. Toss to mix.
4. Pour in orange juice, soy sauce, and honey. Season with salt and pepper. Mix well.
5. Place in the oven and bake for approximately 1 hour, or until chicken is cooked through and squash is tender.

DINNER ON A BAKING SHEET

Diablo Shrimp

This dish is a little spicy and a little sweet. The perfect combination of naughty and nice.

Calories: 272   Fat: 9g   Protein: 28g   Carbs: 15g

Serves: 4

Ingredients:

1 ½ pound medium shrimp, cleaned and deveined
1 cup baby corn
1 pound asparagus, trimmed and cut into 1 inch pieces
1 cup leeks, sliced, whites only
3 cloves garlic, crushed and minced
1 cup orange juice, no sugar added
½ cup apple cider vinegar
1 tablespoon garlic chili sauce
1 jalapeno, quartered
½ cup unsweetened shredded coconut
1 lime, quartered
1 teaspoon salt
1 teaspoon pepper

Directions:

1. The day before, combine all of the ingredients in a large, sealed food storage bag. Make sure ingredients are well blended and place in the refrigerator to marinate overnight.
2. Preheat oven to 375°F.

3. Pour the contents of the bag out onto a lightly oiled, rimmed baking sheet.
4. Toss and spread out to make sure ingredients are evenly distributed.
5. Place in the oven and bake for 20-25 minutes, or until shrimp is cooked and asparagus is crisp tender.

High Protein Roasted Vegetable Medley

Even meatless nights can still be high in protein and low in carbs. This dish takes advantage of some of the most protein-rich vegetables available.

Calories: 432   Fat: 34g   Protein: 12g   Carbs: 18g

Serves: 6

Ingredients:

3 cups Brussels sprouts, halved
2 cups kale, chopped
1 cup sweet potato, cubed
2 cups mushrooms, quartered
2 15 ounce cans garbanzo beans, drained and rinsed
1 cup walnuts, chopped
¼ cup olive oil
1 teaspoon thyme
1 teaspoon oregano
1 teaspoon tarragon
¼ cup fresh grated parmesan cheese

Directions:

1. Preheat oven to 425°F.
2. Spread the Brussels sprouts, kale, sweet potato, mushrooms, garbanzo beans, and walnuts on a baking sheet.
3. Drizzle with olive oil and toss to coat.
4. Season with thyme, oregano, tarragon, and parmesan cheese. Toss to mix.
5. Place in the oven and bake for 35-40 minutes, or until vegetables are tender, tossing once or twice during cooking.

Baked Flounder with Roasted Tomatoes

Seafood is one of the simplest dump meals that you can prepare. This recipe highlights a mellow flavored flounder and brings it new life with lush flavors.

Calories: 414   Fat: 24g   Protein: 36g   Carbs: 12g

Serves: 4

Ingredients:

1 ½ pounds flounder fillets
3 cups plum tomatoes, quartered
1 cup Kalamata olives, halved
1 cup red onion, sliced
3 cloves garlic, minced
¼ cup olive oil
2 tablespoons rice vinegar
1 tablespoon fresh rosemary
1 tablespoon fresh tarragon
1 teaspoon salt
1 teaspoon pepper
1 lemon, sliced

Directions:

1. Preheat oven to 350°F.
2. Lightly oil a baking sheet.
3. Place the flounder, plum tomatoes, olives, red onion, and garlic on the baking sheet.
4. Drizzle with olive oil and rice vinegar. Toss to coat.
5. Season with rosemary, tarragon, salt, and pepper.
6. Top with slices of lemon.
7. Place in the oven and bake for 30-35 minutes or until fish is cooked through and flakey.

Roasted Salmon, Spinach and Warm Leek Salad

This dish is a soul-warming take on the traditional cold salmon and spinach salad.

Calories: 411   Fat: 25g   Protein: 34g   Carbs: 9g

Serves:

Ingredients:

1 ½ pounds salmon fillets, cut into strips
4 cups fresh spinach, torn
1 cup red onion, diced
1 cup leeks, sliced, white parts only
1 cup apricots, sliced
1 tablespoon capers
½ cup walnuts, chopped
3 tablespoons olive oil
1 tablespoon fresh rosemary
1 tablespoon fresh dill
1 teaspoon salt
1 teaspoon cracked black peppercorns

Directions:

1. Preheat oven to 350°F.
2. Lightly oil a baking sheet.
3. Place salmon fillets, spinach, red onion, leeks, apricots, capers, and walnuts on the baking sheet.
4. Drizzle with olive oil and toss to coat.
5. Season with rosemary, dill, salt, and black peppercorns.

6. Place in the oven and bake for 30-35 minutes, or until salmon is pink and flakey.
7. Serve in bowls, garnished with vinaigrette or dressing of choice.

Horseradish Kissed Flank Steak with Roasted Onions

Just a blessing of horseradish gives this dish a bit of a bite. Paired with roasted onions and a savory red wine marinade, this dish is so elegant, no one would ever guess that it was a dump meal.

Calories: 244   Fat: 9g   Protein: 24g   Carbs: 10g

Serves: 6

Ingredients:

1 ½ pounds flank steak
1 tablespoon jarred horseradish
2 cloves garlic, crushed and minced
¼ cup dry red wine
½ cup beef stock
¼ cup Worcestershire sauce
1 medium yellow onion, cut into chunks
1 medium red onion, cut into chunks
2 cups parsnips, cut
1 tablespoon olive oil
1 teaspoon fresh thyme
1 teaspoon fresh oregano
⅛ teaspoon grated lemon rind
1 garlic clove, minced
½ teaspoon salt
¼ teaspoon freshly ground black pepper

Directions:

1. The day before, place the flank steak, horseradish, garlic, red wine, beef stock, and Worcestershire sauce in a sealable food storage bag. Place in the refrigerator to marinate until ready to use.
2. Preheat oven to 375°F.
3. Place the onions and parsnips on a baking sheet. Drizzle with olive oil and toss to coat.
4. Empty the contents of the marinade bag onto the baking sheet, using as much of the liquid as desired.
5. Place in the oven and bake for 40 minutes, or until steak has reached desired doneness.
6. Let stand 10 minutes before slicing.

Conclusion

Eating low carb today means something different than it did a decade ago. Modern low carb eating isn't simply about removing pasta and potatoes from your diet. Now it is all about flavor and enhancing fresh ingredients, with striking new tastes. I hope that within these pages you have found some inspiration for creating easy, delicious low carb recipes that fit into your lifestyle. Preparation does not need to be complex in order for a dish to be a success. The simple 'dump and go' technique used in this book gives you more time to spend enjoying the healthy, active life that you have created.

ABOUT THE AUTHOR

Sarah Spencer, who lives in Canada with her husband and two children, describes herself as an avid foodie who prefers watching the Food Network over a hockey game or NCIS! She is a passionate cook who dedicates all her time between creating new recipes, writing cookbooks, and her family, though not necessarily in that order!

Sarah has had two major influences in her life regarding cooking, her Grandmother and Mama Li.

She was introduced to cooking at an early age by her Grandmother who thought cooking for your loved ones was the single most important thing in life. Not only that, but she was the World's Best Cook in the eyes of all those lucky enough to taste her well-kept secret recipes. Over the years, she conveyed her knowledge and appreciation of food to Sarah.

Sarah moved to Philadelphia when her father was transferred there when Sarah was a young teenager. She became close friends with a girl named Jade, whose parents owned a Chinese take-out restaurant. This is when Sarah met her second biggest influence,

Mama Li. Mama Li was Jade's mother and a professional cook in her own restaurant. Sarah would spend many hours in the restaurant as a helper to Mama Li. Her first job was in the restaurant. Mama Li showed Sarah all about cooking Asian food, knife handling, and mixing just the right amount of spices. Sarah became an excellent Asian cook, especially in Chinese and Thai food.

Along the way, Sarah developed her own style in the kitchen. She loves to try new flavors and mix up ingredients in new and innovative ways. She is also very sensitive to her son's allergy to gluten and has been cooking gluten-free and paleo recipes for quite some time.

Other Books from Sarah Spencer

Shown below are some of her other books.

APPENDIX

Cooking Conversion Charts

1. Volumes

US Fluid Oz.	US	US Dry Oz.	Metric Liquid ml
¼ oz.	2 tsp.	1 oz.	10 ml.
½ oz.	1 tbsp.	2 oz.	15 ml.
1 oz.	2 tbsp.	3 oz.	30 ml.
2 oz.	¼ cup	3½ oz.	60 ml.
4 oz.	½ cup	4 oz.	125 ml.
6 oz.	¾ cup	6 oz.	175 ml.
8 oz.	1 cup	8 oz.	250 ml.

Tsp.= teaspoon - tbsp.= tablespoon – oz.= ounce – ml.= millimeter

2. Oven Temperatures

Celsius (°C)*	Fahrenheit (°F)
90	220
110	225
120	250
140	275
150	300
160	325
180	350
190	375
200	400
215	425
230	450
250	475
260	500

*Rounded numbers

Made in the USA
Lexington, KY
18 March 2016